THE LITTLE BOOK OF
DAD JOKES

This edition published in 2024 by OH
An Imprint of HEADLINE PUBLISHING GROUP

18 20 19 17

Cataloguing in Publication Data is available from the British Library

ISBN 978-1-91161-043-4

Compiled and written by: Malcolm Croft
Editorial: Victoria Denne
Designed and typeset in Avenir by: Tony Seddon
Project manager: Russell Porter
Production: Arlene Lestrade
Printed and bound in China

MIX
Paper | Supporting
responsible forestry
FSC® C104740
www.fsc.org

Headline's policy is to use papers that are natural, renewable and recyclable products and made from wood grown in well-managed forests and other controlled sources. The logging and manufacturing processes are expected to conform to the environmental regulations of the country of origin.

HEADLINE PUBLISHING GROUP
Hachette UK, Carmelite House, 50 Victoria Embankment, London EC4Y 0DZ
Hachette Ireland, 8 Castlecourt Centre, Castleknock, Dublin 15

www.headline.co.uk   www.hachette.co.uk

THE LITTLE BOOK OF
DAD JOKES

SO BAD THEY'RE GOOD

CONTENTS

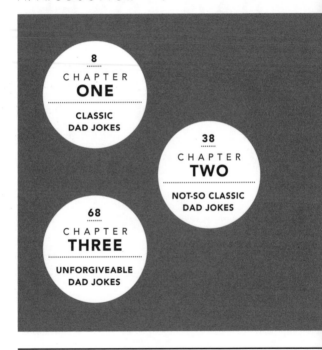

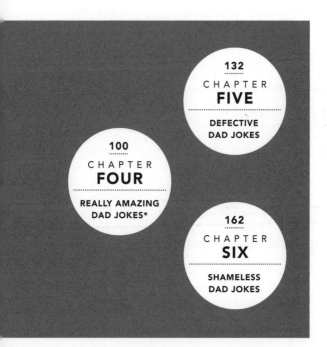

* Just kidding

INTRODUCTION

Dear Dads,

When does a joke become a dad joke?
When the punchline is a parent.
(Apparent – a parent! Get it? Laugh? Exactly.)

The problem with dad jokes is simple: even the good ones are shit.

For decades, maybe even millennia, dads have always believed they were hilarious. No doubt, cave-dads finger-painted puny puns on their cave walls making their cave echo with groans and moans. Ever since, dads have repeated and recycled the same lame quips, puns and one-liners that have been spinning around the world for decades, rarely changing, rarely making anyone happy. In fact, dad jokes create the absolute opposite response to which they are intended, and yet are still laughably called jokes. And therein lies the danger of their sad creation: they are no laughing matter. And, yet, like a thick fart that lingers in the air for hours after its toxicity spritzed the room, dad jokes have *survived*. Worse, they have flourished.

In the past two decades, the reputation of dad jokes has been transformed. Today, dad jokes, like their comedic partner-in-crime, Christmas cracker jokes, are almost revered as an artform, a guilty pleasure, a pure form of comedy – cool, even – a form of joke-telling so bad that it transcends being funny. As fuzzy as that logic sounds, no one seems to be putting a stop to all this dad joke madness. Dads are the only ones in on the "joke" and continue to get away with something that, let's be honest, is tantamount to murder. (And while kids' jokes may be just as bad, kids aren't old enough to know any better. Dads have no excuses.)

Anyway, the dad jokes included in this tiny tome are revered by sad dads all over the world – that's how bad they are. Some of the jokes are old, some of them are new, many are unrepeatable, all of them are worn out and tired and, like dad himself, desperate to be put out to pasture like an old horse you just can't bring yourself to shoot.

If you're a dad, this book is your new best friend: you'll LOL at every single joke. If you've bought this book for your dad, don't panic, we've made the book small for a singular purpose: should the urge to throw it down the toilet arise, it'll disappear in one flush.

The jokes within really are the very best of the very worst. We made sure of it, because we want to wash our hands of this whole dirty affair and never speak of it again. Therefore is the best dad joke book you'll ever read. Sorry.

So, without further ado, why did the toilet paper roll down the hill? To get to the bottom, of course.

And, we're off…

CHAPTER
ONE

CLASSIC
DAD JOKES

"Always obey your parents,
when they are present."

Mark Twain

HOW DID DARTH VADER KNOW WHAT LUKE GOT HIM FOR CHRISTMAS?

He felt his presents!

What do you call a baguette at the zoo?

What do you call an illegally parked frog?

Toad

Why should you not trust stairs?

HOW DOES A PENGUIN BUILD ITS HOUSE?

Igloos it together

Why do fish live in salt water?

What do you call a Frenchman wearing sandals?

What do you call a bear with no ears?

WHY WAS THE SNOWMAN LOOKING THROUGH A BAG OF CARROTS?

He was picking his nose

What do you call it when one cow spies on another?

A steak out!

WHY DO PEOPLE DISLIKE RUSSIAN DOLLS?

Because they're so full of themselves

What's black, white and read all over?

KNOCK, KNOCK!

WHO'S THERE?

DISHES!

DISHES WHO?

22

Dishes a really bad dad joke

What's the difference between roast beef and pea soup?

Why did the golf player wear two pairs of trousers?

Because he got a hole in one

DO YOU WANT TO HEAR A DUSTBIN JOKE?

What do you call a pig that does karate?

Pork chop

How do you make somebody curious?

KNOCK, KNOCK

WHO'S THERE?

DUNUP

DUNUP WHO?

Ew, I hope you haven't!

How do locomotives know where they are going?

Why was the broom late for work?

It overswept

What do you call a million rabbits walking backwards?

A receding hare-line

DID YOU HEAR ABOUT THE CASH MACHINE THAT BECAME ADDICTED TO MONEY?

It suffered from withdrawals

A strip of bacon and an egg walk into a bar.

WHY SHOULD YOU NEVER RUN IN FRONT OF A CAR?

You'll get tired

Why should you never run behind a car?

Which athlete is warmest in the winter?

A long jumper.

WHAT BRAND OF CAR DOES AN EGG DRIVE?

A Volkswagen

CHAPTER
TWO

NOT-SO CLASSIC
DAD JOKES

"Fatherhood is great
because you can ruin someone
from scratch."

Jon Stewart

Why is sea sickness unpleasant?

It comes in waves

WHY DID THE MARATHON RUNNER SPRINT INTO A BARBERS?

WHAT DO YOU CALL AN ALLIGATOR IN A VEST?

An investi-gator

Why did the tomato blush?

Because it saw the salad dressing

How do you turn a duck into a soul singer?

Put it into the microwave until its Bill Withers

WHAT DO YOU CALL A SEAGULL THAT FLIES OVER THE BAY?

A bagel

What is the difference between an angry circus owner and a Roman barber?

One is a raving showman, the other is a shaving Roman

What do Santa's elves listen to as they work?

What do you call a person who counts their chickens before they hatch?

A mathachicken

Did you hear about the Italian chef who died?

He pasta way

NOT-SO CLASSIC DAD JOKES

WHY DID THE OLD MAN FALL IN THE WELL?

Because he couldn't see that well

Why did the invisible man turn down the job offer?

He couldn't see himself doing it

WHAT RHYMES WITH ORANGE?

No it doesn't

Why is Spring embarrassing?

DON'T TRUST ATOMS.

(They make up everything!)

What happens when a frog's car dies?

It needs a jump. If that doesn't work he has to get it toad

HOW DO YOU GET A SQUIRREL TO LIKE YOU?

Act like a nut

Why are cats bad storytellers?

Because they only have one tale

Why was the belt sent to jail?

For holding up a pair of trousers

What's an astronaut's favourite part of a computer?

WHAT DO YOU CALL A MAN WITH A RUBBER TOE?

Why couldn't the bicycle stand up on its own?

Because it was two tired

What do you give a pig when it's poorly?

Oink-ment

WHY DID THE MEXICAN MAN PUSH HIS WIFE OFF A CLIFF?

What was Beethoven's favourite fruit?

Ba-na-na-na

WHAT'S A FOOT LONG AND SLIPPERY?

A slipper.

What do you call it when a hen looks at a lettuce?

A chicken Caeser salad

WHAT DO YOU CALL A MEXICAN WHOSE VEHICLE HAS BEEN STOLEN?

Carlos

CHAPTER
THREE

UNFORGIVEABLE DAD JOKES

"My daughter got me a World's Best Dad mug. So we know she's sarcastic."

Bob Odenkirk

What do you call a deer with no eyes?

No eyed deer.

What do you call a deer with no eyes and no legs?

Still no eyed deer

WHAT'S RED AND BAD FOR YOUR TEETH?

A brick

What did the horse say after it tripped?

"Help! I've fallen...I can't giddy-up!"

TWO ANTENNAS MET ON A ROOF, FELL IN LOVE AND GOT MARRIED.

The ceremony wasn't much, but the reception was excellent

Did you hear about the dad who lost his job at the calendar factory?

He took a couple of days off

Did you hear about the two thieves who stole a calendar?

They each got six months

What do you call a can opener that doesn't work?

HOW MANY TICKLES DOES IT TAKE TO TICKLE AN OCTOPUS?

Tentacles

WHAT DID THE CLEANER SAY WHEN HE JUMPED OUT OF THE CLOSET?

WHAT DO YOU CALL A SMALL MOTHER?

What's at the bottom of the ocean and shivers?

Why did the man with one hand cross the road?

To get to the second hand shop

WHAT WORD IS ALWAYS SPELLED WRONG IN THE DICTIONARY?

Wrong

Why is the word "drool" so much fun to say?

It just rolls off the tongue

Why didn't the astronaut come home to his wife?

He needed his space

WHY ARE THERE GATES AROUND CEMETERIES?

Because people are dying to get in!

WHAT STREETS DO GHOSTS HAUNT?

Are all pools safe for swimming?

It deep ends

WHAT DO YOU CALL A ONE-EYED DINOSAUR?

Did you hear the one about the magic tractor?

It was driving down the road when it suddenly turned into a field

Where do you learn to make ice cream?

WHAT DOES SANTA SUFFER FROM IF HE GETS STUCK IN A CHIMNEY?

Claus-trophobia

What do you call a rabbit that has fleas?

WHY DO BEES HAVE STICKY HAIR?

Because they use a honeycomb

Why can't two elephants swim at the same time?

Because they only have
one pair of trunks

Why was the leaf collector wealthy?

He was raking it in

What do you call a decomposing whale?

Why did the chicken go to the séance?

To get to the other side

WHAT KIND OF EXERCISE DO LAZY PEOPLE DO?

CHAPTER
FOUR

REALLY AMAZING
DAD JOKES*

"The hardest thing
about being a parent is these
goddamned kids."

Andy Richter

* Just kidding

WHY DID THE EMPLOYEE GET FIRED FROM THEIR JOB AT THE BANK?

Somebody asked for their balance to be checked, so they pushed them over

Why do cow-milking stools only have three legs?

HOW MANY EARS DOES SPOCK HAVE?

Three. The left ear, the right ear, and the final frontear!

Why don't animals play poker in the jungle?

DID YOU HEAR ABOUT THE DAD WHO WAS TERRIFIED OF ELEVATORS?

He started taking steps to avoid them

Three fish are in a tank.

One fish asks the others,
"How do you drive this thing?"

Two cannibals are eating a clown.

One says to the other:
"Does this taste funny to you?"

WHAT DID ONE OCEAN SAY TO THE OTHER OCEAN?

Nothing, they just waved

HAVE YOU EVER TRIED TO READ A BOOK ON ANTI-GRAVITY?

It's impossible to put down

Did you hear the joke about the obsessive chess players in a hotel reception, talking about how good they are?

They were chess-nuts boasting in an open foyer

Why don't ants get ill?

Because they have anty-bodies

What do you call a horse that moves around a lot?

DID YOU HEAR ABOUT THE GREEDY CLOCK?

It went back four seconds

What did the drummer call his twin daughters?

What's the dumbest animal in the jungle?

A polar bear

What does a lawyer wear to court?

A lawsuit!

What sound does a witch's car make?

Broom Broom

Why doesn't an elephant care what you call them?

It's irrelephant

WHAT DID THE GRAPE DO WHEN HE GOT STEPPED ON?

It let out a little wine

Where did Napoleon keep his armies?

DID YOU HEAR ABOUT THE DAD WHO HAD HIS LEFT SIDE CUT OFF?

He's all right now

WHAT DO YOU CALL A COW WITH NO LEGS?

Why are elevator jokes so good?

They work on many levels

How does a meteorologist go up a mountain?

HOW DO YOU CUT THE OCEAN IN HALF?

With a sea-saw

What did the doctor say to the patient who couldn't stop gloating?

"Take this cream and don't rub it in"

WHAT DO YOU CALL A PONY WITH A COUGH?

A little hoarse

HOW DO YOU MAKE A TISSUE DANCE?

How does Darth Vader like his toast?

On the dark side

What did the duck say when it bought lipstick?

CHAPTER
FIVE

DEFECTIVE
DAD JOKES

"The worst part about being a
parent is when one of your
kids farts and you have to pretend
it wasn't cool."

Rob Delaney

Why didn't the sesame seed stop and say hello?

It was on a roll

What did the fisherman say to the magician?

WHY WAS THE ROBOT EXHAUSTED AFTER HIS ROAD TRIP?

He had a hard drive

Which bear is the most condescending?

How do you get a farmer's daughter's attention?

A tractor

What do mathematicians say to the person who invented the number zero?

What do you call a camel with no humps?

Humphrey!

WHY DID THE NOSE MOVE SCHOOL?

Because it was getting picked on

IF IRON MAN AND SILVER SURFER TEAMED UP, WHAT WOULD THEY BE CALLED?

Alloys

What's a computer's favourite snack?

What happened to the dad who ate a dictionary?

It gave him thesaurus throat he's ever had

WHAT'S LIFE WITHOUT GEOMETRY?

What did the late tomato say to the other tomatoes?

Don't worry, I'll ketchup

DID YOU HEAR ABOUT THE DAD WHO SLEPT LIKE A LOG?

He woke up in the fireplace

WHAT'S GREEN AND HAS WHEELS?

Grass. I lied about the wheels.

What do you call a psychic short person who has escaped from prison?

Why don't molluscs run?

In case they pull a mussel

WHAT DO YOU CALL AN OLD PERSON WITH REALLY GOOD HEARING?

What does a flower say when it makes a mistake?

"Oopsy-daisy"

WHAT FISH WORK IN HOSPITALS?

WHAT DID THE POLICEMAN SAY TO HIS BELLY BUTTON?

"You're under a vest!"

Why should you feel scared for calendars?

Why did the student eat his homework?

Because the teacher told him
it was a piece of cake!

What is brown, hairy and wears sunglasses?

What kind of tree fits in your hand?

A palm tree!

HOW DOES THE MOON CUT HIS HAIR?

WHAT SOUND DOES A NUT MAKE WHEN IT SNEEZES?

Cashew

What do you get if you eat Christmas decorations?

CHAPTER
SIX

SHAMELESS DAD JOKES

"Dad always thought
laughter was the best medicine,
which I guess is why several of us
died of tuberculosis."

Jack Handey

What do you call a dad with no body and no nose?

Nobody knows

You know what the loudest pet you can get is?

A trumpet

WHY DID THE SCARECROW WIN AN AWARD?

He was outstanding in his field

WHAT DID THE BUFFALO SAY WHEN HIS SON LEFT FOR SCHOOL?

What do you call a fish with no eye?

Fish

How do you interrogate a cheese toastie?

WHY CAN'T YOU HEAR A PTERODACTYL GO TO THE BATHROOM?

Because the pee is silent

What do you call a man who can't stand up?

WHY DON'T CRABS DONATE?

Because they're shellfish

Ever tried to eat a clock?

Did you hear about the festival fire?

It was in tents

What did the child pirate get on his school report card?

What's Forrest Gump's password?

1forrest1

Did you hear the joke about the world's worst thesaurus?

WHY IS SIX SCARED OF SEVEN?

Because seven ate nine and ten

WHAT DO YOU CALL A BOOMERANG THAT DOESN'T COME BACK?

A stick

How do you light up a football stadium?

With a football match

WHAT DO YOU CALL A MAN WITH A SEAGULL ON HIS HEAD?

Cliff

Did you hear about the dad who accidentally handed his wife superglue instead of lipstick?

She still isn't talking to him

WHAT DO YOU CALL A DOG THAT CAN DO MAGIC TRICKS?

A Labracadabrador

A red ship collided with a blue ship.

All the sailors were marooned

An apple pie in Jamaica is £1.50, a cherry pie in Barbados is £1.60 and a mince pie in Trinidad is £1.80.

What should you call a woman whose voice sounds like an ambulance?

DID YOU HEAR ABOUT THE EXPLOSION AT THE CHEESE FACTORY?

There was nothing left but de brie

WHAT DO YOU CALL A COW WITH A TWITCH?

Beef jerky

Why did the wedding cake need a tissue?

Because it was in tiers

I ONCE BOUGHT A DOG FROM A BLACKSMITH.

As soon as I got it home, it made a bolt for the door.

What do you call a donkey with three legs?

A wonkey

WHAT DO YOU CALL A FAKE NOODLE?

An impasta